Essential Care of
Chameleons

FROM THE EXPERTS AT
ADVANCED VIVARIUM SYSTEMS™

By Philippe de Vosjoli

THE HERPETOCULTURAL LIBRARY™
Advanced Vivarium Systems™
Irvine, California

Karla Austin, *business operations manager*
Jarad Krywicki, *editor*
Erin Kuechenmeister, *production editor*
Nick Clemente, *special consultant*
Design by Michael Vincent Capozzi
Cover design by Vicky Vaughn
All photos by Philippe de Vosjoli except where otherwise indicated
Rachel Rice, *indexer*

Cover photography by David Northcott

The photographs in this book are courtesy of: David Northcott, pp. 9, 33, 36, 53, 56; Chris Estep, courtesy of Reptile Haven, p. 38; Liddy Kammer, p. 49; © 2004 www.clipart.com, pp. 7, 13; and © 2004 www.photos.com, pp. 30, 55.

LCCN: 96-183295
ISBN: 1-882770-61-7

An Imprint of BowTie Press®
A Division of BowTie, Inc.
3 Burroughs
Irvine, CA 92618
www.avsbooks.com
(877) 4-AVS-BOOK

We want to hear from you. What books would you like to see in the future? Please feel free to write us with any comments on our AVS books.

Printed in Singapore
10 9 8 7 6 5 4 3 2 1

CONTENTS

CHAPTER 1

GENERAL INFORMATION

Chameleons are Old World lizards that hail from the family Chameleonidae. Half of the 135 species of chameleons hail from the island of Madagascar, while most others range throughout Africa; a few species are also found in the Middle East, Europe, and Asia. The smallest chameleon is *Brookesia minima*, from Madagascar, which reaches a total length of an inch and a half as an adult, making it one of the smallest lizards in the world. The largest chameleons are Oustalet's, Parson's, and Meller's chameleons, all of which can exceed 2 feet in total length; the world's largest chameleon, the Oustalet's, occasionally grows more than 30 inches.

Characteristics

The vast majority of chameleons have eyes capable of moving independently of one another, but this trait is not unique to chameleons. (The exceptions are Brookesines chameleons, which have limited ability for independent eye

The small and live-bearing Tanzanian dwarf chameleon is hardy as long as it is kept in appropriate temperatures, and receives light supplementation (no more than once a week).

movement.) Their most unique feature is the fused prehensile digits of their hands and feet, which form pincer-like appendages; no other living lizards in the world have evolved this characteristic.

Also characteristic of chameleons is a helmet-like portion of the head defined by parietal and lateral crests, called a casque, after the French word for helmet. Chameleons' casques evolved, in part, to accommodate shifts in facial structure caused by large, forward positioned eyes, and a shortening of the snout and the muscles required for eye movement. Some species have evolved large casques that may serve adaptive functions, such as thermoregulation (a means of controlling body temperature) or a secondary sexual characteristic. Research has yet to confirm the notion that some species large casques serve as a surface for water condensation, thereby giving them an additional water source.

Chameleons also have a prehensile tail, which helps keep them stable when climbing trees and shrubs, and allows them to anchor to surrounding branches. In most situations, it is strong enough to prevent the lizards from falling.

The other well-known feature of chameleons is their projectile tongue, which allows them to capture insects and other prey from a distance—in certain species, the tongue's range can be more than twice the body length! Though other lizards use their tongue to capture prey, chameleons' tongues are far more specialized for this task than those of other species.

Most chameleons have laterally flattened bodies. This allows them to move more freely among tree branches and shrubs, to thermoregulate more effectively in arboreal environments, and to better hide themselves among their surroundings.

Chameleons and the Law

All chameleons except members of the genera *Brookesia* and *Rampholeon* are listed under Appendix II of the Convention on International Trade in Endangered Species (CITES), meaning that CITES permits are required if you wish to transport the animals between countries. In addition, several countries also protect chameleon species. Consult the pertinent wildlife regulatory agency before collecting, importing, or exporting any chameleon. In the United States, a number of states regulate the ownership of true chameleons, and Hawaii prohibits the importation of chameleons. Other states, such as Maine and Massachussets (these two states have some of the most peculiar amphibian and reptile laws in the nation), have permit requirements for the ownership of chameleons.

Longevity

Though many consider chameleons to be short-lived, the various species have a wide range of life histories and life expectancies. The following are longevity records of captive specimens from some of the popular chameleon species:

- Flap-necked chameleon (*Chamealeo dilepis*): Four years
- Veiled chameleon (*C. calyptratus*): Eight years for a male; Five and a half years for a female
- Fischer's chameleon (*Bradypodion fischeri*): Three years from young adults; likely four to five years if raised from hatching
- Panther chameleon (*Furcifer pardalis*): Nine years for males; Five years for females
- Carpet chameleon (*Fur. lateralis*): Three years
- Parson's chameleon (*Calumma parsonii*): Eight and a half years from large mature adults; likely ten years or more if raised from hatchlings
- Jackson's chameleon (*C. jacksonii*): Nine years
- *Brookesia stumpfi*: Three years
- Armored chameleon (*Bro. perarmata*): Two years from adults; likely this species has a potential longevity of five years

Taxonomy

The taxonomic system proposed by Klaver and Bohme, which emphasized hemipenis and lung morphologies, is increasingly used by herpetologists and chameleon enthusiasts. Based on that system, Chameleonidae are divided into two subfamilies. The subfamily Brookesinae includes members of the genera *Brookesia* (from Madagascar) and *Rampholeon* (from Africa). The subfamily Chameleoninae includes the Malagasy genera *Calumma* (e.g., Parson's chameleon) and *Furcifer* (e.g., panther chameleon); and the African genera *Bradypodion* (e.g., Fischer's chameleon) and Chamaeleo (e.g., veiled chameleon, Chamaeleo calyptratus). The latter genus also includes the subgenus *Trioceros* (e.g., Jackson's chameleon).

If you are purchasing your first chameleon your best choice is one of the popular captive-bred species, such as veiled chameleon.

CHAPTER 2

SELECTION AND ACCLIMATIZATION

Before You Buy

Before purchasing a chameleon, first decide what species interests you. If you have no experience with chameleons, your best choice is one of the popular captive-bred beginner species, such as veiled and panther chameleons. Before deciding on a species, research the climatic conditions of your area; if you live in a hot, dry area, a species that requires high relative humidity will be costly to set up and may not be the best choice. If you live in a cool and wet area, then species that prefer a more moderate relative humidity may not be the best suited for your conditions.

A free-roaming Moroantsetera male panther chameleon in a pet store.

Next, consider how much space you want to dedicate to keeping a chameleon. Any medium or large species of chameleon will take up a significant portion of a room if kept indoors under optimal conditions. If you do not have enough space, rethink your choice. You also need to decide whether it is important for your chameleon to display a certain degree of responsiveness; some species are far more responsive than others. If the longevity of your pet is a concern, remember that males of many egg-laying chameleon species tend to be longer-lived in captivity than females. The best pet species for beginners are panther and veiled chameleons, particularly captive-bred males.

Captive-bred or Wild-caught?

As a general rule, captive-bred chameleons are a more dependable purchase than those that are wild-caught, because they are less likely to be parasitized or stressed. If you purchase them when young, you will also have a good estimate of their age.

However, captive-raised specimens are not always a better choice than imports. For example, the great majority of captive-bred Jackson's chameleons do not reach maturity. In contrast, healthy, imported subadult Jackson's chameleons tend to be hardy (only if their care requirements are met). Among larger species of chameleons, such as panther chameleons, captive-bred babies are generally hardier than

Since Hawaii closed its exports, the live-bearing Jackson's chameleon has become difficult to obtain. It is an ideal species for those living in cooler, more humid climates.

wild-caught adults, provided they are given the proper conditions and diet. Obviously, if it is difficult for you to meet the dietary requirements of a baby chameleon, choose a healthy looking, imported young or subadult chameleon instead. Several species, such as *C. montium*, which are tiny and delicate as babies, are more difficult to raise and maintain than healthy imported adults. The safest bet is to buy young and healthy-looking chameleons, but not necessarily tiny hatchlings. The young hatchlings tend to be more delicate, and do not make suitable pets for inexperienced keepers; experts even have trouble raising certain species.

Selecting a Healthy Chameleon

A simple visual inspection will improve the odds of selecting a healthy specimen, but it has limited effectiveness. As a general rule, do not select the largest and most impressive chameleon; instead, select a half-grown or small specimen (very likely of a young age). If you are purchasing a medium or large species, choose an animal with a body length of around three inches. For inexperienced owners, animals of this size are generally easier to maintain than babies.

As part of your selection process, make sure that your chameleon meets the following criteria:

- Both eyes should be open and active, and appear to be equal size. Do not purchase an animal that has sunken eyes.
- The body should have rounded, smooth contours, and the outlines of skeletal structures should not be visible.
- In imports, the outline of its hip-bones may be apparent. Though this may be due to lack of proper feeding, it may be a sign of disease or high parasite infection. Try to avoid animals with this problem.
- The limbs and digits should appear even, and be free of lumps or swelling.
- The chameleon's skin should not have dry, crusty patches or small nodules.
- Ask to handle the animal, then allow it climb on you. A healthy chameleon gives the impression of a strong grip for its size, and will tend to be active. Look at the vent

area while it is climbing to make sure there are no caked feces or fecal smears. If present, they could be a sign of parasites or gastrointestinal (GI) disease.

Animals per Enclosure

Many chameleon species, including the popular veiled, panther, flap-necked and Oustalet's chameleons, are asocial outside of the breeding season and fare best when kept singly, except for short breeding introductions. As a general rule for most species, do not keep males together in the same cage or, if kept loose, in the same room.

There are several species that can be kept in male/female pairs or trios (one male with two females), but only when kept in large enclosures or on indoor trees. I have successfully kept Fischer's, four-horned, Jackson's, Parson's, carpet, Natal dwarf, Tanzanian dwarf, and armored chameleons in pairs or trios. With some species, I have noticed instances of apparent social pair bonding (e.g., the animals always sleep next to each other). Experts do not recommend mixing species, but some keepers have had success with certain combinations. If you plan on keeping more than one animal, closely observe your collection to determine whether the species can be safely kept together, and whether they are stressed under such conditions.

Acclimating Wild-caught Chameleons

Most imported chameleons are caught as mature adults, which means that their potential longevity is limited compared to that of an immature animal. In addition, many wild-caught animals are stressed, heavily para-sitized, and dehydrated, and they present a significant risk of loss for potential buyers, especially within the first few months of captivity.

When acclimating imported chameleons, first set up the new animals in individual enclosures. Using a dripper two to three times a day will allow the animal to rehydrate, and offer them food twice a day (see Feeding). Deparasitize imported chameleons with fenbendazole (Panacur, Hoechst-Roussel) to remove nematodes. Noted veterinary doctor Tom Boyer, DVM, recommends four treatments at two week intervals, though some veterinarians recommend other regimens, such as smaller doses given for five consecutive days. You can also use ivermectin and metronidazole (Flagyl) to deparasitize your chameleons. Consult an experienced veterinarian experienced for advice on anthelmintics and the regimen best suited to your chameleons. If your animals show signs of listlessness or illness, they may also require antibiotic treatment; consult an experienced veterinarian to determine the proper course of treatment.

Quarantine

If you already keep chameleons or other lizards, it is critical that you quarantine new purchases in individual cages, in a room completely separate from your other animals, for at least ninety days. Meller's chameleons should always be kept in a room far away from all other chameleons, preferably in another building. If you do use hygienic quarantine procedures, coccidiosis, cryptosporidiosis, and fatal viral infections can decimate your collection. Coccidiosis, in particular, has become increasingly common among veiled chameleons.

To minimize the spread of disease, tend your quarantined acquisitions after you look after the rest of your collection. Wash your hands thoroughly with an antibacterial soap after handling newly acquired chameleons or tending to their enclosures. More than one chameleon expert has faced the consequences of not quarantining a supposedly captive-raised panther, veiled, or Jackson's chameleon. You have been warned.

During quarantine, closely observe an animal for signs of illness, including failure to eat or drink, listlessness, runny feces, worms, weight loss, gaping and forced exhalations, nodules on the skin, eye problems, and unusual swelling. If you notice anything wrong, consult an experienced veterinarian for the proper treatment.

CHAPTER 3

SEXING AND THE LIFE STAGES OF A CHAMELEON

Sexing

With most species, if one looks for the correct signs, it is fairly easy to determine whether an animal is male or female. The most obvious sign in many species is that males have an elongated bulge at the base of the tail, formed by the inverted hemipenes (the reproductive organs of male chameleons). In addition, because many chameleons are territorial, they have secondary sexual characteristics that allow the sexes to recognize each other at a distance. The most widespread of these characteristic is sexual

Many collections of veiled chameleons are now past their tenth generation breeding.

dichromatism, differences in color and pattern between males and females. For example, male panther chameleons are typically brightly colored, while females have a rather drab appearance. On the other hand, female carpet chameleons typically have brighter coloration than males, particularly when gravid (pregnant).

Sexual dichromatism can also be temporary and may be indicative of an individual's reproductive condition. A female veiled chameleon that is ready for breeding has a specific color and pattern scheme, while a non-receptive, gravid female has a different high-contrast combination of color and pattern, which clearly informs a male that she is not open to sexual advances.

Another common secondary characteristic is sexual dimorphism, a difference in size and form between males and females. In many species, such as panther, Oustalet's, and veiled chameleons, males are larger than females. Several complexes of chameleons have sexually dimorphic casques. High-casqued (*C. hoehnelii*) and veiled chameleons are two of the best known examples of this, and males of both species have a significantly larger casque than females. In other species, sexual dimorphism can include other structures, such as horns, rostral processes, or dorsal and caudal crests. Male Jackson's chameleons, for example, have large supraocular horns; male Fischer's chameleons and Parson's chameleons have pronounced rostral processes; and male four-horned and crested chameleons have large dorsal and caudal crests. Some species of chameleons, such as Meller's and armored chameleons, have minor sexual differences and can be difficult to sex. With other species, such as the spiny chameleon (*Fur verrucosus*), the sexes look so different that they appear to be totally different species.

The Life Stages of Chameleons

Like most lizards, chameleons go through four basic life stages. Understanding these stages is important in the process of becoming a good herpetoculturist. The four broad life stages can be categorized as follows:

I.   Pre-birth/embryonic

II. Juvenile/subadult
III. Sexually mature adult
IV. Old age

Chameleon breeders concern themselves with the first stage, because proper management, such as nutrition of females and incubation conditions, impacts egg and embryonic development. The second stage, the juvenile/subadult stage, is characterized by an initially small size and high body surface-to-volume ratio, followed by rapid growth and a progressive decrease in the surface-to-volume ratio. The chameleon's purpose at this stage is primarily to feed and grow. Intraspecies aggression and territorial behaviors are minimal, which means that, with most species, chameleons can be kept together during this time. However, larger animals eventually have a competitive advantage over smaller ones and, if kept in close quarters, end up intimidating them. In several species of chameleons (e.g., flap-necked chameleons) the subadult stage is characterized by increased territorial and aggressive behaviors, but no breeding behaviors.

Most vertebrates typically grow to a size where they can successfully reproduce, and then their bodies start to expend energy resources toward reproduction rather than growth. This also happens to chameleons during the third stage, sexual maturity, characterized by sexual behaviors, territoriality, intraspecies aggressive and defensive displays, and aggression. During the third stage, the chameleon starts to focuses on reproduction—sex was of no concern before. Once a chameleon reaches this stage, its growth rate slows down considerably, particularly among females. In several species of chameleons, excess feeding and supplementation at this stage may lead to obesity among males and to females that produce unusually large numbers of eggs. For example, wild veiled chameleons often lay only one clutch each year, with usually less than twenty-six eggs per clutch. In captivity, however, female veiled chameleons lay up to four clutches a year, with sixty or more eggs per clutch. This is likely a direct result of feeding management and the temperature of the animal's enclosure.

In many species of lizards, egg production declines after a couple of years. Preliminary research also shows this to be true for many chameleons. The last stage, old age, is seldom reached by chameleons, but, when it is attained, it may be characterized by infrequent or absent egg production, limited activity, reduced feeding, and various subtle external signs of aging, such as raised scales or wrinkly skin. To extend an animal's life span at this stage, cut back on the amount of food you feed it and reduce the caloric content of its diet. Good herpetoculturists make adjustments in the feeding schedule and the enclosure's environmental conditions to accommodate the requirements of each life stage.

CHAPTER 4

HOUSING

Indoor Tree Setups

ndoors, you can keep all adult medium and large chameleons, including *C. calyptratus*, *C. dilepis*, *B. fischeri*, *C. melleri*, *C. pardalis*, *C parsonii*, *and C. quadricornis*, without a cage, on *Ficus benjamina* trees placed near windows that receive sunlight for a few hours a day. Put the potted trees in saucers, and light the area with a spotlight clamped on a photographic

Indoor trees, placed near a window and supplied with a spotlight, are the most effective setups for keeping a chameleon indoors. Make sure children do not handle or pester chameleons on these setups.

lamp stand or placed in a wall or ceiling fixture near the top branches of the tree. The light serves as a source of heat. Be very careful when positioning the bulbs so that you minimize the risk of fire. Keep the lights away from flammable materials, such as drapes, and place them at least 12 inches from all branches and perches. Firmly anchor the fixture so that it does not to fall. You can provide ultraviolet (UV) radiation by hanging fluorescent fixtures with UV-B generating reptile bulbs, but an economical alternative is to open a screened window (keep the screen down) when the weather is good to allow your chameleon exposure to natural sunlight (optimal UV exposure is between 10 AM and 2 PM).

Hang a drip bag in the tree so that your chameleons have a source of water. Make sure the water drips through the tube onto leaves, and flows toward the base of the pot. This method also waters the tree, and excess water collects in the saucer. Offer your chameleons crickets that have had their hind legs pinched (to prevent the prey from escaping) and other prey items in a food container anchored in tree branches. Remember that, for most species, a chameleon's tongue extend about one and a half times its total body length, so the depth of the feeding containers must be significantly less than that distance to be effective.

There are a few other requirements for this system to work. First, you must keep the tree in a closed room. When entering the room, do so carefully so that you don't accidentally strike a wandering chameleon with the door. Always look down to make sure you do not accidentally step on and crush your chameleon, and keep cats, dogs, and other pets out of the chameleon's room. Make sure that the window near the chameleon's enclosure does not receive intense, hot sun all day long. This can overheat a room to such a degree that it will cause the death of your chameleon. If necessary, plant shade trees or shrubs outside the window to prevent prolonged intense sunlight. Constantly evaluate your methods and monitor the setup regularly. Generally, this type of setup is one of the best systems for long-term indoor care of large chameleon species.

Some UV-B light gets through glass panes, but excess heat is a problem with windows facing the southwest. Open screened windows during nice weather to expose your chameleons to unfiltered sunlight.

In warmer climates, walk-in wire, aviaries are ideal enclosures for chameleons.

Chameleon Trees

Ficus benjamina, which is available in supermarkets as well as plant nurseries, is the best choice when keeping chameleons indoors. The standard variety is ideal for most medium and large chameleons, and smaller specimens are suitable for babies. Dwarf umbrella plants also create good indoor trees, but you must bend their stems because their vertical growth does not make good perching sites. In warmer areas of the U.S., *Ficus benjamina*, privet, mulberry, hibiscus, and a number of fruit trees make good outdoor trees for your chameleon. For obvious reasons, avoid trees with large leaves or spiny branches.

Because a wide range of chemicals are used in horticulture, mist the leaves of all recently purchased plants with a mix of water and liquid dish detergent, then to hose down the plants with plain water to clean off the pesticide residues.

Some keepers use climbing plants wrapped around branches as an alternative to indoor trees. Pothos is the best choice for this purpose, as it is hardy and grows quickly. For small species or juveniles, certain *Nematanthus* species work well.

Enclosure Size

Enclosure size is not a consideration for those using the indoor tree method of keeping, but other enclosures for large chameleons should have a perimeter that is at least six times the chameleon's total length, and a height that is at least twice the chameleon's total length. These are rough guidelines, and variations are possible (e.g., less height but greater length). With smaller species and babies, enclosures equivalent to 20- or 30-gallon aquaria work well. With these animals, larger enclosures are not necessarily better because the size permits ready dispersal of insect prey following introduction.

Screen Cages

Many specialists advocate screen or wire mesh cages, deeming them the perfect chameleon enclosures. Although screen cages are ideal for many species, herpetoculturists have suc-

Three four-horned chameleons inhabit this screen cage, which uses a polystyrene foam bottom to support a *Ficus benjamina* tree. The three drip systems on top of the cage are watered twice a day, in the late morning and at 3 PM. The owners only place this cage in direct sunlight when the temperature is below 82° F, and the tree provides adequate shade.

cessfully raised chameleons using a variety of methods. The greatest limitation of all-glass enclosures is size; large all-glass enclosures are heavy and expensive. Most sizes sold in pet stores are generally too small to accommodate small trees and shrubs or to provide the height and space required by the popular chameleon species. Thus, the great advantage of screen or welded wire cages is that they are relatively light and economical for their size. They are usually have the height necessary to house small trees or shrubs, and because the walls are screen or wire, chameleons can use the vertical surfaces for climbing and moving about. The "claw-at-the-sides" behavior sometimes performed by chameleons in exceedingly small glass tanks is not usually seen in screen enclosures.

In general, commercially available screen-sided enclosures are best for small- to medium-sized chameleons, although very large screen enclosures can be special ordered for large species. When possible, I recommend keeping the larger chameleons loose on indoor trees or in large, plastic-coated welded wire cages.

Glass Enclosures

Although some keepers do not think that glass-walled enclosures with screen tops are suitable for chameleons, they are incorrect. Certain species require high relative humidity and fare quite well in large, all glass enclosures. The reduced ventilation helps to maintain an optimal level of humidity.

Generally, the humidity-loving Cameroonian species, such as the four-horned and montane chameleons, fare well in large (4- to 6-foot long) glass-sided, screen-top enclosures. Carpet chameleons have been bred and raised, and have good long-term success, in glass-sided enclosures. Jackson's, veiled, and panther chameleons have been successfully raised and kept long-term in larger glass-sided enclosures with screen tops. As could be expected, the small leaf-litter chameleons of the genera *Brookesia* and *Rampholeon* also do well in glass-sided enclosures with screen tops. In addition, many breeders raise baby chameleons in glass-sided vivaria, because it reduces the amount of baby crickets that escape and keeps the crickets readily available for feeding. For species accustomed to high humidity (such as mountain chameleons), reduced ventilation is essential.

Some herpetoculturists say that chameleons become stressed in glass enclosures because they see their reflection in the glass, but I believe their claims are greatly exaggerated. Ultimately, the best enclosures for large chameleon species are large enclosures, no matter what type, but keeping larger species loose on indoor trees is an even better choice.

Basking Cages

Many people keep their chameleons in indoor tree setups or screen cages, but use a smaller, portable screen cage to provide the lizards with sunlight several times a week. In order to put a plant or tree in a portable screen-sided cage, cut a section of thick polystyrene board that fits securely on the plastic floor frame; this allows you to put a planted tree inside the cage and move it back and forth without risking damage to the screen floor. In addition to my movable screen cages, I have walk-in aviaries in my backyard that I use to allow large species to bask.

Cats, Raccoons, and Other Predators

My first long-lived pair of Jackson's chameleons was mutilated and killed by a raccoon. They had fared well indoors, and I later decided to put them in a welded wire cage outdoors. One evening, a raccoon seized their limbs through the sides of their cage and chewed them off. Any chameleon kept in large, outdoor mesh cages may be a victim of this kind of attack. Many other predators, including foxes, skunks, opossums, and dogs, will also try to eat chameleons. Around the home, the greatest enemies of free-roaming lizards are cats, which attempt to kill lizards at virtually every opportunity.

Raising Baby Chameleons

For the first four to eight weeks, baby chameleons of many species will fare well in 12-inch tall glass-sided enclosures with small leaved, potted plants, such as dwarf cultivars of *Ficus benjamina* or Nematanthus (do not use standard *Ficus benjamina* or pothos plants). Keep the enclosure floor bare, and light no more than a third of the enclosure with a small incandescent bulb, which will serve as a heat source. Also provide a full-spectrum or high UV-B fluorescent reptile bulb running the length of the enclosure.

I have had unusually good success raising baby veiled and panther chameleons using a small 50-watt halogen light placed on one side of an enclosure, within two inches of the screen top. These bulbs, even with the UV filter (do not remove it or you will burn your chameleons), apparently emit small amounts of UV-B light. We've also had success using small, 35- to 50-watt halogen bulbs as the exclusive source of heat and light when raising these species to a length of 12 inches, and then transferring them to other caging.

To supply water, mist the leaves and sides of the enclosure lightly two to three times a day. Never spray water directly on babies. This stresses them and, if sprayed at night, can cause them to become too cold, risking respiratory infection and death. Feed the young chameleons with small, seven- to ten-day-old crickets, depending on species and size of the chameleons, or supplemented fruit flies. Offer the food twice a day.

Once weekly, transfer the babies to an outdoor, screen-sided basking cage that includes shade-offering plants. Baby chameleons will die quickly if they do not have shelter from the sun or if exposed to direct sunlight while in a glass or plastic enclosure. Many hobbyists raise baby chameleons in screen cages from start to finish, but this may not be the optimal rearing system for many species.

Substrate

For chameleons kept in large cages, newspaper is the best substrate because it is inexpensive and easily replaced. If you use an indoor tree setup, place plastic sheeting under the potted plants to help preserve your floor. The plastic sheeting is also easily washed and replaced. In outdoor cages, the ground of most areas is adequate as long as it is mostly soil. In glass-sided cages, either bare floors, newspaper, or fine, moistened potting soil work well. With most Brookesines, use a moistened potting soil with a leaf litter cover to provide the necessary conditions. Avoid potting soils with perlite (white granules) which can be accidentally ingested.

CHAPTER 5

WATER AND RELATIVE HUMIDITY

Relative Humidity

I n his *Royal Natural History* (published in 1896), Richard Lydekker noted that the distribution of chameleons was, in part, determined by relative humidity. For wild chameleons, the primary effect of relative humidity occurs in the evening when temperatures drop, causing water droplets to form on surfaces such as leaves, thereby providing a source of drinking water despite the absence of rain. Relative humidity also affects the rate of evaporative water loss that occurs during respiration.

With the proper relative humidity, a chameleon's skin looks and feels supple and velvety. In captivity, relative humidity should ideally range between 70 and 80 percent for most species. This level can be assessed with a measuring

Hand watering large chameleons is a good way to be sure that they are getting enough water. The animals are attracted to the shining ball tip and the dripping water.

device called a hygrometer. Inexpensive hygrometers are available in the reptile trade, and more expensive and accurate instruments can be bought from biological supply houses. Chameleon species from savannahs and arid climates require humidity levels between 60 and 70 percent, and many rainforest species fare best at 75 to 85 percent humidity. As a rule, a relative humidity greater than 85 percent can lead to problems, because it greatly assists bacterial and fungal growth, particularly if the high humidity is combined with heat. If you keep your chameleons in an area with extremely high humidity levels, good ventilation is essential.

If the relative humidity in a room is too low, use a cool-air humidifier or electronic humidifier to raise the humidity. Always use clean water and regularly wash and disinfect the water container as instructed. When using a cool-air humidifier, partially open a window or door (if chameleons are caged) so there is some ventilation.

Ventilation

Most chameleons don't fare well in saturated humidity or in rooms or enclosures without good air flow. If kept in a glass enclosure, chameleons need good ventilation; the entire top should be made of screen and at least half of this top needs to be left free of lighting fixtures or other coverings.

To create a drip container, poke a small hole through the bottom of a deli cup and place it above the leaves in a chameleon's enclosure. Make sure you use high-quality water.

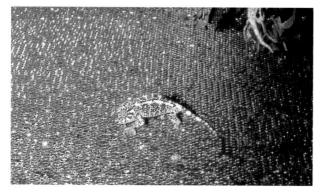

Water

Chameleons recognize rain and dew droplets when the light reflects off their surface, and recognize moving water by its bubbles, wavelets, and ripples. Generally, they have a difficult time recognizing water, although a few species, such as the armored chameleon, readily drink from shallow water dishes.

Drip Systems

Drip systems are the best water source for most adult chameleons, though they are not suitable for babies and exceptionally small species, such as those of *Brookesia* and *Rampholeon*. Several types of drip systems are currently available, including the favored medical enteral feeding bag. Whatever system you choose, adjust the drip rate to fall at one drop every one or two seconds. Place the end of the drip tube in an area easily accessible to your chameleon; specimens quickly learn to drink from the end of the tube. Every two weeks, clean and disinfect the container and outlet with a 5-percent bleach solution. Ideally, you should replace drip systems every few months to maintain hygiene levels.

Drip Containers

You can use a deli cup with a hole punched in the bottom or containers drilled to accommodate an aquarium air valve as drippers. However, your chameleon has to wait until the water falls onto a leaf before it can drink, so you must carefully position the dripper so that droplets fall and form on leaves.

These systems work well in heavily planted setups, but tube outlets are generally more effective means of keeping your chameleons hydrated. As with other drip systems, place a container below the dripper to collect water and empty it each day.

Misters

Misters, connected to a plumbing system and set on a timer, are an excellent way to hydrate chameleons in outdoor or indoor enclosures with proper drainage. Direct the misters toward easily accessible areas of foliage, and the chameleons will drink off the leaves. Make sure that you do not over-mist the enclosure, and that relative humidity levels remain in the proper range.

Rodent Water Bottles

Sipper bottles normally used with rodents are ideal for hand-watering chameleons. The lizards are attracted to both the water droplets falling from the tip and the reflection of the metallic ball inside the tip. To assure that larger chameleons are getting enough water, occasionally offer them water from this type of bottle. Put the ball tip near (or just above) the tip of their snout and gently squeeze out a few drops. When initially presented with the water bottle, a chameleon may shy away, but this does not always mean it is not thirsty. Keep the bottle in place and continue dripping for several minutes. Chameleons often come back and begin drinking once they have determined that they are safe. My wife waters our chameleons with a drip system early in the day, and often hand-waters them with a rodent water bottle later in the afternoon.

Spray Bottles

You can use hand sprayers to mist leaves and as the primary method of watering baby chameleons. Never spray babies directly; instead, mist the surrounding foliage and the sides of the enclosure. If you use a spray bottle with larger chameleons, lightly spray the edges of their mouth (not their eyes) to elicit drinking behavior. Once they open their mouth, continue to gently spray the water into it until they are satisfied. Like rodent water bottles, spray bottles make a good secondary watering method.

When you have many enclosures or animals to mist, a pump sprayer greatly facilitates the process. However, algal and bacterial scum tend to build up in the water holding tank of pump sprayers, so you need to wash it with antibacterial soap and disinfect it with a 5 percent bleach solution at least once a month. Rinse it thoroughly before each use.

Water Containers

Brookesia perarmata will drink out of shallow water containers of still water, and I offer a water dish to all *Brookesia* and *Rampholeon* species. Make sure to keep no more than a quarter-inch of water in the containers.

An all-screen chameleon cage with a potted plant, and a drip bag on the top.

CHAPTER 6

HEATING

Temperature and Extra Heat

Chameleons are ectotherms, meaning they depend on environmental temperatures to regulate their body temperatures. In nature there can be significant differences in temperature in a single environment, depending on the ecology of a particular habitat. For example, during the day, temperatures under the

Keep the basking site temperature for veiled chameleons between 86–90° F.

shade of foliage can be more than 10 degrees Fahrenheit (F) cooler than those of areas receiving direct sunlight. In weather extremes, underground burrows or shelters provide protection from cold or heat. Environments with both moisture and breeze allow evaporative cooling. In the wild, a chameleon moves between these different microclimates to maintain the necessary body temperature.

In captivity, you must provide conditions that allow a chameleon to warm up to its optimal body temperature or move to a shaded and cooler area. For species that inhabit warm climates, such as panther, veiled, and Oustalet's chameleons, this means providing a basking site heated to 90° F at the accessible area closest to the spotlight. For species accustomed to cooler temperatures, such as Jackson's, Tanzanian dwarf, sailfin, four-horned, and Johnston's chameleons, this basking site should be around 84° F, and the ambient enclosure temperatures should be in the 70s F.

If you fail to provide an area where the chameleon can achieve its optimal temperature, it may cause metabolic bone disease or kidney disease, and will weaken the chameleon's immune system, eventually resulting in its death.

Cooling

Several chameleon species cannot tolerate high temperatures, including Jackson's chameleon, many Cameroonian forest-dwelling species, and a number of Malagasy chameleons. If the daytime temperatures in your area exceed 84° F, a cooling system or air conditioner is essential. In an emergency, when your animals are overheated, spray them with a cool water mist and aim a low-speed fan at their enclosure. This may work for a brief period, but, if the temperature remains high, they will need an air conditioner. In general, babies are significantly less tolerant of heat-induced stress than adults.

Air conditioners tend to reduce relative humidity, so you may also need to purchase a cool-air humidifier for the chameleon's room. In warm climates, air conditioners or evaporative cooling systems are essential to the survival of your chameleons.

Night

In most situations, you should turn off all lights during the night. Chameleons appear to have the best long-term survival rates when there is a nighttime drop in temperature. Most species tolerate nighttime temperatures in the low 70s F and even those in the high 60s F. Montane species are even able to tolerate temperatures in the 40s F for short periods, and the hardiest species may survive a light frost, but such conditions should be avoided.

Thermometers

The only way to assess the temperature of a room or basking site is to use a thermometer. Inexpensive stick-on thermometers are available in many pet stores, and glass thermometers are available in hardware stores and pharmacies. Most serious hobbyists prefer digital electronic thermometers with external probes for "outside" readings. By placing a probe at an enclosure's basking site, you can get a continuous reading of the temperature.

Spotlights

Indoors, a spotlight is the best localized heat and light source available. Place it in a reflector-type fixture with a ceramic base, and put it over the top of the cage, above the screen or wire lid. Make sure that the bulb does not make direct contact with the screen. If you are using an indoor tree setup, affix the light fixture to a photographic lighting stand and aim it at the setup.

The inexpensive reflector fixtures with built-in switches sold in many hardware stores will work for months, but the switches eventually burn out, and will need to be replaced. Reflector fixtures with a ceramic base and no switch, and flood light fixtures with a cord switch, will last much longer. Be careful when selecting the spotlight bulb; if the wattage is too high, the bulb will cook a chameleon in close confines. For small tanks, use a 60-watt bulb, at most.

When placing your spotlight, make sure it is securely positioned away from any flammable material. Poorly positioned and poorly anchored light fixtures are fires waiting to happen. Pets or children may bang into fixtures, causing insecure setups to tumble to the ground, and poor placement can set curtains on fire. To be safe, always keep a working smoke detector in rooms with heating devices or spotlights.

UV Bulbs

When you are unable to expose your chameleon to proper sunlight conditions, whether due to temperature extremes or inclement weather, a UV-B generating reptile bulb will allow them to synthesize vitamin D_3, which they need to survive. Experts also recommend UV-B lights when rearing baby chameleons indoors.

A number of UV bulbs are sold by reptile stores, but keepers are often unsure about what bulb to use. For a long time, the Vita Lite bulb, which generates UV-A and UV-B light, was the only bulb available on the market. Its UV-B output is relatively low, but if you supply several bulbs, and the animals can get within 6 inches of the light, they are effective. Though there are now many other bulbs available, they do not all provide the necessary light, and you need to make sure the bulb lives up to its claims before purchasing it. The best way to find out what works is to ask a respected herpetologist or a well-known chameleon keeper. To assure the efficiency of your lighting, replace full-spectrum and fluorescent UV-B bulbs every six to eight months.

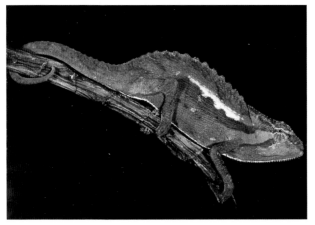

Wiedersheim's chameleon is a very pretty species occasionally imported from Cameroon, and best kept in temperatures in the upper 70s F during the day.

Sunlight

Sunlight, nature's heat source, is the most effective means of allowing arboreal reptiles to raise their body temperature. With many species of chameleons, it also allows the animals to synthesize vitamin D_3, which facilitates the absorption of calcium, and assists in other metabolic functions.

Though chameleon experts continue to emphasize the importance of exposure to sunlight in a chameleon's vitamin D_3 synthesis, each species of chameleon is the product of a different set of evolutionary determinants, and there is likely a wide range of sunlight requirements between species. Some species, for example, appear better adapted to utilize dietary vitamin D_3, while others need little exposure to sunlight to fulfill their bodies' requirements. The question is: How much sunlight is necessary?

Humans require relatively little exposure to sunlight, and chameleons are likely very similar; exposing them to a few hours of natural sunlight each week should allow them to synthesize all the vitamin D_3 they need. If they get at least two hours of sunlight each week, you do not need to use UV-B bulbs in their enclosure. However, sunlight also may have psychological benefits, and full-spectrum bulbs will provide these benefits.

Much more species-specific research needs to be done in this area. So, until proper information is available, continue to expose your chameleon to at least a few hours of sunlight each week, and/or provide them with high-output UV-B reptile bulbs and spotlights.

Proper Sunlight Exposure

Do not expose chameleons to sunlight through glass. In addition to filtering out most of the beneficial UV radiation, glass can magnify the heat intensity of the light, causing a greenhouse-like effect and cooking your chameleon. Instead, use screen or wire mesh cages. In an indoor screen-house, you can place a piece of glass over a small section of the screen roofing to create a warmer basking spot in cool weather, provided your chameleons have a way to avoid this area.

If you keep your chameleons in a room with southern exposure, carefully monitor its temperature. When the windows are closed, rooms with southern exposure can overheat. To regulate the amount of sunlight entering the room, place a shade cloth over the window, or plant shrubs or trees outside the widow.

Chameleons need a shaded area whenever they are in direct sunlight. By moving back and forth between the shaded and lit sections of an enclosure, the chameleons keep their body temperature at the desired level. Without a shaded area, your chameleons may not survive.

CHAPTER 7

FEEDING

When to Feed

Offer food to your chameleon every day; you can skip a day without causing any harm, but do not make a habit of it. During certain times of the year, some chameleon species even refuse food or feed sporadically for extended periods. As long as your chameleon maintains good weight and remains healthy and alert during this time, do not be concerned.

Diet

Most chameleons primarily feed on insects, although some also feed on snails, and larger species will eat small vertebrates (displaying a definite preference for other lizards).

A flap-necked chameleon striking a cricket.

Crickets

Though the myth that crickets are not a good staple diet for chameleons persists in herpetoculture, many chameleon species fare well on a mostly cricket diet. The problems normally associated with cricket diets are usually the result of poor cricket husbandry, not because crickets are a bad dietary item. I have seen Jackson's chameleons kept for more than eight years on a primarily cricket diet, and I own a Parson's chameleon who has lived for more than seven years on the same feeding regimen.

Keep feeder crickets in clean, well-ventilated containers to prevent mold growth, and feed them greens, grated vegetables, and sliced fruit before feeding them to your chameleons. Mold toxins (such as aflatoxins) that accumulate in crickets fed grain-based diets have been cited as a possible cause of liver disease and a shortened life span among chameleons. Proper cricket husbandry, including clean, mold-free containers and plant-based diets, will help prevent this possibility.

Superworms

In small amounts, this oversized variation of the superworm is a suitable component of the diet of larger chameleons. Feed grated vegetables, apple slices, and leafy greens to the superworm before feeding them to your chameleon. Superworms tend to be fatty, so offer them in limited quantities.

Wax worms and Silkworms

Wax worms (*Galleria melonella*), which are actually wax moth caterpillars, can be purchased by mail order, and are suitable for medium and large species of chameleon when fed in small amounts. If you feed too many to your chameleon, they will often be regurgitated.

Keepers sometimes offer small amounts of silkworms (*Bombyx mori)*, the caterpillars of mulberry silk moths, to their chameleons to vary their diet, but I have found that they are problematic, causing constipation and possible impaction in some specimens. Many chameleons will eat them ravenously, later showing signs of digestive distress and then refusing to eat them again.

This tame, two-year-old male Oustalet's chameleon prepares to strike a super-worm. This impressive species continues to be underrated by the herpetological community.

Roaches

Biological supply companies sell several species of roaches, and chameleon specialists often raise them as food for their animals. The most popular roaches cultured by hobbyists are Madagascan hissing cockroaches, which do not make good chameleon food except in their smaller, immature stages, and roaches from the *Blaberus* genus. Some states have laws that control certain commercially raised species, so check your state laws before purchasing them.

Roaches are opportunistic feeders, which means that their gut content can be varied by altering their diet. In nymph form, roaches make a good diet for chameleons; some reports show that larger roaches' spiny legs abrade a chameleon's gastrointestinal tract, possibly leading to fatal infections or choking. Because of these problems, I recommend that you do not feed adult roaches to your chameleons. Wingless and nymph roaches can be kept in deep, smooth-sided feeding containers and fed to your chameleon when appropriate. Because roaches tend to burrow and hide, they do not make a good food choice for animals kept in vivaria with soil or bark substrates.

Flies

If gut-loaded (fed nutritious food) prior to feeding, flies make a good supplemental item for your chameleon's diet. Use only flies that were commercially raised and purchased as maggots from an insect supplier. Keep any feeder flies in a screen-sided fly-raising container; if these are not available, pupate them in a deli cup with a mesh top held in place by rubber bands.

Offer your feeder flies a high-quality diet, including such items as powdered milk, fish flakes, baby cereal flakes, and moistened cat and dog food. As with other feeder insects, they should be fed a varied diet. Unless you carefully control and evaluate the nutritional content of your feeder flies, do not use them as the primary food source for your chameleons.

To transfer flies to a chameleon's enclosure, clip a nylon stocking with its toe cut off to the fly jar, and guide the flies into the chameleon's cage. If the flies don't move, remember that they are attracted to light and will likely fly towards a bright light. You can put the flies in your refrigerator for about ten minutes to slow their response time.

Lizards and Pink Mice

Larger species of chameleons probably get some of their vitamin D_3 by ingesting other vertebrates, primarily other lizards. The largest chameleons may even feed on small birds and featherless nestlings. I have seen wild panther chameleons catch and eat day geckoes and other chameleons, and have seen a captive Meller's chameleon attempt to eat four-horned chameleons and other small species.

Large captive chameleons readily eat green anoles and various geckoes, and these foods, as well as pink mice, make suitable diet items once every two to four weeks (not more often). Such food provides a wide range of vitamins, minerals, proteins, and essential fatty acids, and in time, many chameleons will learn to take it from food dishes. Several species of gecko are particularly easy to breed and make a decent food source (my apologies to gecko fans).

However, even with such an easily replenished source, vertebrates should only make up a small portion of a chameleon's diet.

Snails

The edible gray snail (*Helix aspersa*), which is now farmed and has been introduced in a number of areas, makes a good addition to the diet of chameleons originating from humid forests. Parson's, Jackson's, and four-horned chameleons all readily feed on active snails. Small, dime-sized snails with thin shells make the best feeder animals.

Feed your snails mustard greens and soaked dry dog food for at least three days before feeding them to your chameleons in order to clear their stomach of potentially toxic plants. Even following this procedure, uncooked snails may still harbor harmful parasites and toxins. Snail shells contain large amounts of calcium and their flesh is high in protein but low in fat and carbohydrates.

Plant Matter

At least one species of chameleon (veileds) eagerly eats plant matter as an adult. Other species occasionally feed on plant matter, and most incidentally ingest plant matter while hunting insects. Triangular bite marks on the tender leaves of your veiled chameleon's *Ficus benjamina* tree indicate that it has begun feeding on plants. To increase the probability that it does this, you need to make it hungry. Offering crickets every other day rather than every day often does the trick.

Once a chameleon starts feeding on plant matter, it will eat romaine and mustard greens, as well as sections of green fruits like grapes and kiwis. It may even eat certain flowers, such as hibiscus. Be sure to remove uneaten plant matter because dried up pieces can become lodged in the chameleon's throat, causing it to choke. In time, plant matter may comprise more than 40 percent of the food consumed by an adult veiled chameleon. The lower caloric content of a partially herbivorous diet may help reduce reproductive rate and increase the life span of captive chameleons.

A veiled chameleon feeds from a tall, plastic deli cup. These inexpensive containers are tall enough to prevent prey from escaping and are easily replaced.

All chameleons will consume plant matter, but you may first need to feed it to your feeder insects for most species. If you gut-load your feeder insects with plant matter, the chameleons will ingest beneficial nutrients, thereby adding to their general health.

Feeding Baby Chameleons

If you expect the birth of baby chameleons in your collection, make sure you have a source of small insects to use as food. Generally, you can order pinhead and one-week-old crickets by mail or special order them from your pet store, and they will usually arrive within a week. Week-old crickets are a good size for most hatchling chameleons, and large, flightless fruit flies (*Drosophila hydei*) make a good supplemental and backup diet. Very small baby chameleons will eat smaller flightless fruit flies (*Dro. Melanogaster*) after hatching. Never offer a baby chameleon prey with a length greater than the length of its head.

Fruit flies are easy to raise, but, if you need a good supply, you must set up breeding containers several weeks before you need them. *Drosophila melanogaster* live for almost two weeks and *Dro. Hydei* live for three to four weeks.

Vitamin and Mineral Supplementation

Few areas of chameleon keeping are as controversial as proper supplementation. Herpetoculturists agree that both excessive and insufficient supplementation are both problematic, but very little research has been conducted in the area, and no available supplement is designed specifically for chameleons.

With larger chameleons kept indoors, many keepers have had success with the following formula: combine one part finely ground calcium carbonate and/or calcium gluconate powder with two parts of a regular reptile powdered multi-vitamin/mineral supplement that contains vitamin A and vitamin D_3. Lightly dust feeder insects before each feeding by adding a small pinch of the vitamin mix to a jar containing the feeder insects, then gently swirling the jar until the insects are lightly coated with the supplement. Make sure that the insects are lightly dusted, not caked with the mix. In other words, do not add too much supplement to the jar—it can lead to toxic levels of vitamins and other nutrients, resulting in disease or death.

The proper supplementation regimen depends on a number of factors, including diet, husbandry methods, and the species being kept. Though each situation calls for different methods, the following general guidelines will help you get started:

- For fast-growing, large species (such as veiled and panther chameleons), lightly supplement one feeding each day.
- For medium-sized species, such as flap-necked and four-horned chameleons, supplement feedings three or four a week.
- For small species that grow slowly, such as Tanzanian dwarf and Weidersheim's chameleons, lightly supplement one feeding per week.
- If you regularly expose your chameleon to sunlight, use a vitamin/mineral supplement containing vitamin D_3 only once a week. At other feedings scheduled for supplementation, use a supplement that does not contain vitamin D_3.

- For gravid female chameleons, use a supplement mix made up of two parts calcium and two parts vitamin/mineral supplement.
- Some keepers only use calcium supplements and have good results because they also gut-load their crickets with a variety of nutritious foods. If you use this approach, make sure to offer a varied diet to the feeder insects. Give the crickets a source of beta-carotene (such as cooked yam or grated carrot), vitamin C (orange slices), and B vitamins (yeast flakes), and foods that contain vitamin A and vitamin D_3. Most hobbyists that use this method also expose their chameleons to sunlight, and tend to be fairly experienced keepers.

These crickets have been placed in a feeding cup and lightly dusted with a vitamin/mineral supplement.

Food Size

Appropriate prey insects should be nearly as long as the width of a chameleon's head, though chameleons occasionally eat prey as long or longer than their head. Apply this rule to all dietary staples (crickets, flies, etc.) in order to prevent problems.

Offering Food

When feeding chameleons in screen cages and glass-sided enclosures, many keepers simply place insects in the cage or in small deli cups set inside the cage. Keepers with large, walk-in cages or indoor tree setups typically feed their chameleons by hand or place prey in food-storage containers or deli cups to help prevent escape. When hand-feeding your animal, merely hold out the prey between your fingers until the chameleon eats it.

Variety

Some chameleon keepers consider a varied diet to be essential to a chameleons health, while others think that crickets alone do not constitute a healthy diet, but I have seen many captive chameleons live long, healthy lives on a primarily cricket diet, and do not side with such ideas. Crickets raised under healthy conditions, fed a varied diet, and properly supplemented make a good diet for your chameleon. If you can vary this diet with other insects or prey items, all the better, but do not feel that you need to constantly vary your chameleon's food.

CHAPTER 8

BREEDING

This book primarily deals with proper chameleon husbandry, not breeding, which is too complex to be covered in a book this size. Below is a brief overview of captive breeding of chameleons, but you should refer to the AVS title *Care and Breeding of Chameleons* for more detailed information.

Most chameleons lay eggs, but a significant number of African species are live-bearing, including several members of the *Bradypodion* genus and some members of the *Trioceros subgenus*. Most species become sexually mature by twelve months of age, but a few, such as Parson's chameleons, take longer to reach maturity, and in captivity a few popular species, such as veiled and panther chameleons, become sexually mature in as few as five months. Amazingly, carpet chameleons can reach sexually maturity after only three months. The health consequences of reaching sexual

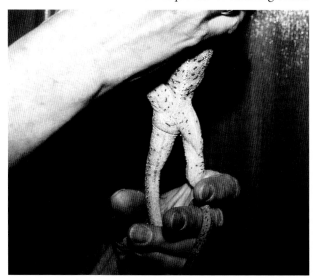

Male panther chameleons have a clearly visible hemipenal bulge.

Panther chameleon
eggs carefully
unearthed from the
base of a tree.

maturity at a young age are relatively minor for males, but can be extremely consequential for females, who expend a great deal of energy and nutrients during egg production.

In captivity, heavy feeding and high supplementation levels can cause female panther and veiled chameleons to produce abnormally large numbers of eggs with abnormal frequency, thereby shortening their lifespan and increasing the risk of egg-binding (see Diseases and Disorders) and other complications. Large, frequent clutches tax a female's calcium stores and cause a calcium crash (acute hypocalcemia) after the eggs pass through the shell gland. Calcium deficiency, whether chronic or acute, with or without hypocalcemia, is commonly associated with failure to lay and egg-binding. Keep this in mind when creating a feeding regimen for breeding chameleons.

How to Breed Chameleons

To begin breeding your chameleons, you must have at least one healthy male and female. Do not attempt to breed weak, thin, or sickly animals. Some species breed best after a period of rest (called brumation); in the U.S., many species will rest, feeding less often and not breeding, from late fall to early spring. Other species can breed year-round, as long as extended daylight, optimal temperatures, and abundant food are available. Some chameleons, such as four-horned and Fischer's chameleons, can be kept in pairs all year, while others, such as veiled and panther chameleons, are best kept separately except during breeding. A few species can be kept in groups.

Most chameleons breed easily. If the female is receptive, breeding usually occurs soon after a male is introduced into her enclosure. Non-receptive females quickly make males aware that they are not interested; remove the male within twenty-four hours if this is the case, and then try the introduction later. Several egg-laying species, including panther, veiled, and Oustalet's chameleons, adopt a gravid/non-receptive coloration after a successful breeding.

After copulation, most egg-laying species gestate for about a month, but because females can store sperm, it is not always possible to accurately determine the time-course of fertilization and is therefore difficult to predict the time of birth or egg laying. It also can be difficult to determine a female's reproductive stage. Generally, females appear swollen when ovulating. In egg-laying species, after fertilization and after the eggs pass through the shell gland, the outline of individual eggs is visible on the female. At this time, you can palpate individual eggs through the female's abdominal wall, and should place a container with 8 to 24 inches of compacted, moist, sandy soil inside the female's enclosure.

Add a small potted ficus on top of the soil because most female chameleons prefer to lay their eggs at the base of trees or shrubs. The root ball of the ficus also provides a source of moisture and some insulation for the eggs. As the babies hatch, they will climb up the tree and hide from potential predators. Failing to provide a proper egg-laying site can contribute to the risk of egg-binding.

After eggs laying, female chameleons need ample food and water. Once you are confident that a female has finished laying, carefully dig up the eggs and place them in an incubation chamber.

Incubation

Proper egg incubation tends to fall into three categories:

- Incubate eggs of many montane and forest species, such as Parson's, four-horned, and Johnston's chameleons, at 68–74° F.
- Incubate veiled, panther, flap-necked, and Oustalet's chameleon eggs at 74–84° F. Other similar species may also fall into this category.
- Eggs of some species from areas with extended dry and/or cool season (such as the common chameleon) may require a diapause (a period of dormancy) during incubation. Experts recommend a cool period before normal incubation temperatures to stimulate development of these eggs.
- Incubate the eggs of chameleons from cool, moist areas in moistened vermiculite. Use either vermiculite, vermiculite/perlite mix, or pure perlite when incubating eggs laid by species from drier areas. Place 1.5 inches of the incubating medium in an incubating container, such as a plastic food storage container, deli cup, or incubator base, and make sure the container has a few small air holes. Bury the eggs on their side, leaving about one-third exposed to allow you to monitor them. Depending on the species and incubation conditions, eggs will hatch in 45 days (some *Brookesia*) to as long as two years (Parson's chameleons).

CHAPTER 9
NOTES ON POPULAR SPECIES

Each species of chameleon has different care requirements depending on a number of factors, including distribution, size and longevity. Refer to the following information for more specific care requirements for your species:

Panther Chameleon (*Fur. pardalis*)

Distribution
Panther chameleons are widespread in northern Madagascar.

Size
Males reach up to 20 inches in total length.

A male panther chameleon from Ambanja.

Sexing
Males are much larger than females and have a well-defined lateral white line running the length of their body. They are also more colorful and have hemipenal bulges.

Longevity
Females live from one to five years, and males usually survive for two to seven years.

Acclimation
Many imports are parasitized with filarial worms (see Diseases and Disorders for treatment), and some may be infected with nematodes or other internal parasites. Younger, smaller animals have less chance of being infected, and make a better option for purchase.

Care
Indoors, keep adults on *Ficus benjamina* trees that receive some light from screened windows. Keep ambient daytime temperatures between 76–82° F and the basking site temperature around 90° F. Ambient nighttime temperatures should drop to 60–76° F. For other concerns, use the general principles listed in this book.

Carpet Chameleon (*Fur. lateralis*)

Distribution
Carpet chameleons hail from Madagascar.

Size
Males grow to a total length of 6 to 7 inches.

Sexing
Males are slightly larger than females, with more slender bodies. In addition they have a more green coloration and visible hemipenal bulges.

Longevity
Carpet chameleons are short-lived in the wild, but they can live up to three years in captivity.

Selection
If you purchase an import, always pick one of the smallest animals available. When available, captive-bred specimens are the best choice; they tend to be hardy, grow quickly, and fare well in captivity.

Care
The commonly imported small form of the carpet chameleon is usually collected near the capital of Madagascar, Tananarivo, located in the country's central highlands. It fares best when kept in fairly cool temperatures ranging in the 70s F during the day and dropping into the 60s F at night. This form cannot tolerate temperatures above 85° F.

The large form, the major carpet chameleon, is collected in the hot west coast and fares best in warmer temperatures. Keep this species in ambient daytime temperatures in the low to mid 80s F, with a basking site that reaches up to 90° F.

Carpet chameleons fare best as single pairs in screen- or glass-sided enclosures. My experience has shown that all-glass enclosures with full-spectrum lighting and a spotlight are the best choice for this species. Make sure specimens kept indoors receive at least one or two hours of sunlight each week. In outdoor enclosures, place a layer of sandy soil over a drainage layer planted with small trees and shrubs.

Flap-necked Chameleon (*C. dilepis*)

Size
Depending on the subspecies and population, flap-necked chameleons vary between 9 to 14 inches. The larger forms are quite impressive and their size often surprises those who have not seen a large chameleon.

Sexing
In most subspecies, males have small tarsal spurs and tend to be more slender than the females. Males also have hemipenal bulges, and, in some species, have a vivid orange coloration on the interstitial skin of their throat.

Acclimation
Deparasitze flap-necked chameleons with fenbendazole. In my experience, these animals are quite hardy and fare well in captivity. One of my imported females, obtained as a large adult, has been in my collection for more than twenty months.

Care
Use the standard guidelines listed in this book.

The Fischer's chameleon (male shown) is a hardy species currently imported from Tanzania. Although it breeds readily, few hobbyists have successfully incubated clutches the full term.

Fischer's Chameleon (*Brad. fischeri*)

Distribution

There are six subspecies of Fischer's chameleon, hailing from Kenya and Tanzania. Three subspecies are commonly imported from Tanzania, the large *B. f. fischeri*, the medium-sized *B. f. multituberculatus*, and the small *Brad. f. taventanus*.

Size

The larger imported subspecies can reach a total length of 15 inches.

Sexing

In all but one subspecies, males have large rostral processes. They are also more slender bodied, with hemipenal bulges and more distinctive colors and patterns.

Longevity

I have kept imported adult specimens for three years.

Acclimation

Some imports are healthy upon arrival, while others have signs of internal parasites and should be treated accordingly.

Care

Fischer's chameleons prefer ambient daytime temperatures in the mid to high 70s F, but will tolerate slightly warmer conditions. Keep the basking site between 82–85° F, and drop ambient nighttime temperatures into the 60s F. Small subspecies fare well in pairs, even in small cages, but pairs of larger specimens need large cages to minimize stress.

Four-horned Chameleon (*C. quadricornis*)

Distribution
Four-horned chameleons originate in Cameroon.

Sexing
Males are larger, with distinctive snout horns and large dorsal and caudal crests.

Care
This hardy species fares best in ambient daytime temperatures in the mid to upper 70s F, but will tolerate slightly warmer temperatures. The basking site should reach 85° F. Lower the nighttime temperature into the 60s F. This species also requires a relative humidity between 70 to 80 percent. Water your four-horned chameleons twice a day and exposure them to sunlight every week, or keep them under high-output UV-B reptile bulbs. Always provide shade. Keep these chameleons in pairs or trios in large cages or indoor trees. Sailfin chameleons (*C. montium*), which are less hardy and more sensitive to heat, fare well under similar conditions.

Jackson's Chameleon (*C. jacksonii*)

Distribution
Jackson's chameleons hail from East Africa, but most U.S. specimens originated in Hawaii, where the subspecies *C. J. xantholophus* was introduced.

Size
This species grows up to 13 inches long.

Sexing
Males have three large horns and are slimmer than females.

Male Jackson's chameleons have three large horns and are slimmer than females.

Care

Keep Jackson's chameleons in screen or welded wire cages, or on indoor tree setups. They prefer ambient daytime temperatures of 76–82° F, with drops into the 50s and 60s F at night. Supply a basking site with a temperature of 85° F so that they can thermoregulate. Regularly expose Jackson's chameleons to a source of UV-B light, preferably sunlight, and keep the relative humidity of their enclosure between 70 to 80 percent, with good ventilation. They feed on insects but also eat snails and flies, and large specimens will eat pink mice when offered (no more than twice a month). Keep pairs in walk-in cages, otherwise keep them singly.

Oustalet's Chameleon (*Fur. oustaleti*)

Distribution

Oustalet's are widely distributed throughout Madagscar.

Size

Oustalet's are one of the three largest chameleons in the world, and are the longest. Males from Morondava sometimes exceed 30 inches in total length.

Sexing

Males are larger, exhibit hemipenal bulges, and have larger casques and distinctive coloration. Females are smaller, usually green, and heavier bodied. When gravid, females exhibit a high-contrast red color pattern.

Acclimation

All imports tend to be heavily parasitized and may require up to four fenbendazole treatments (see Diseases and Disorders). Among imports, mortality rates also tend to be high, so babies, when available, are the best choice for prospective owners.

Care

Like panther chameleons, there are several geographical forms of Oustalet's chameleons that have significantly different husbandry requirements. Species hailing from the same climate as panther chameleons require the same care conditions. The large western form (with a contrasting black and white casque) is accustomed to more arid environments and requires ambient daytime temperatures in the 70s F, and a basking site heated to 90–95°.

Meller's chameleon is one of the largest chameleons, and a carnivorous species that readily feeds on smaller lizards and birds. Unfortunately, imports can harbor viruses deadly to themselves and many other chameleons.

In addition to insects, Oustalet's chameleons feed on lizards as adults. I believe such prey is an important component of a proper diet for this species. During my studies, I have seen a large, wild male Oustalet's chameleon eat a subadult panther chameleon. They also relish geckoes.

Meller's Chameleon (*C. melleri*)

Some of the largest chameleons, these awesome, but problematic, beasts are only for experienced keepers.

Size

Meller's chameleon can exceed 2 feet in total length.

Sexing

Meller's chameleons have no obvious external signs to distinguish the sexes. Males may be larger and heavier bodied than females.

Acclimation

Imports of this species are notorious for having a high mortality rate, and carrying viruses capable of decimating a chameleon collection. In general, the best course of success is to start with captive-hatched juveniles. Segregate males from other chameleons, because they try to eat small species and attack larger ones. A single bite from a Meller's chameleon can infect an animal with a fatal virus.

Care

This species can be kept using the same guidelines listed for panther chameleons, using indoor tree setups or large cages. They are the most aggressively carnivorous chameleon species, and particularly relish other lizards, including chameleons.

Tanzanian Dwarf Chameleon (*C. rudis*)

Distribution

There are four subspecies, and imports typically originate in Tanzania.

Size
These chameleons grow up to 6 inches in length.

Sexing
Females are a uniform green, with heavier bodies than males. Males have hemipenal bulges and distinctive coloration.

Acclimation
To date, few have attempted to establish this species in captivity. Nonetheless, it has many features which make it an ideal pet; it is attractive, small, and hardy, and bears live young.

Care
Keep ambient daytime temperatures in the mid to high 70s F. These chameleons enjoy temperatures in the low 80s F, but become stressed if conditions rise higher than 85° F, and overheating is a common cause of death. Expose specimens to sunlight each week, and keep them at a relative humidity of 60–70 percent. Keep males separately, or, if you have a large cage, in male/female pairs or trios (one male, two females). Babies can be difficult to raise, but many problems may be caused by over-supplementation. Lightly supplement any young and make sure they have proper exposure to a source of UV light. Babies reach sexual maturity after ten months. All ages relish crickets and flies.

Veiled Chameleon (*C. calyptratus*)

Distribution
Veiled chameleons hail from the border between Yemen and Saudi Arabia.

Size
Specimens grow up to 24 inches in total length.

Sexing
Males are larger, with larger casques and hemipenal bulges.

Adult male veiled chameleons can be recognized by their high casque, brighter coloration, hemipenal bulge, and tarsal spurs.

Longevity

Males can live up to eight years; females rarely live longer than five.

Acclimation

This is the only chameleon firmly established in herpetoculture, and many collections are now past their tenth generation breeding. If you want a good, responsive pet, purchase a young veiled chameleon, raise it in an environment with frequent human activity (a kitchen, for example), and interact with it frequently once it has a body length of about 2 inches. This means taking time for two or three short sessions (five to ten minutes) to get it to climb on your finger, hand-feed it, and later to allow itself to be carried and climb from hand to hand. As the chameleon gets larger (3 to 4 inches) allow it to rest on your shoulder for longer periods of time.

Care

House veiled chameleons in large cages or indoor tree setups. Keep the basking site temperature between 86–90° F.

Because veiled chameleons develop very quickly, they are susceptible to metabolic bone disease, meaning that you must properly supplement their diet with calcium and vitamin D_3. Make sure to reduce the amount of vitamin D_3 if they have access to a source of UV-B light.

Veiled chameleons enjoy feeding on plant matter, and, when hungry, will begin nibbling on vegetation. Once they have begun feeding on plants, feed them insects every other day, alternating these feedings with dishes of plant matter (see Feeding for more details). The lower fat content of this diet will help your veiled chameleon live longer.

CHAPTER 10

DISEASES AND DISORDERS

Before you seek veterinary services, find out if there is a good chameleon veterinarian in your area; local herpetological societies should be able to help you with this endeavor. Inexperienced veterinarians often do more harm than good for chameleons, and they cost a great deal of money. Good chameleon veterinarians are rare, but they will give you an honest opinion about your animal's condition and will often be able to save its life. Most veterinarians can perform basic fecal exams and check for parasites, but you should leave treatment advice to experienced reptile veterinarians. Regardless of the problem, isolate sick chameleons in a room apart from other chameleons, and always quarantine new animals. The following brief overview of common medical problems may help you diagnose and treat your chameleon.

Dehydration
Signs of dehydration include dry, wrinkled skin; sunken eyes; listlessness; weakness; and weight loss. If the chameleon is still relatively active and alert, offer it water or Pedialyte several times each day. If your animal is too weak to drink on its own, consult a qualified veterinarian.

Metabolic Bone Disease
Afflicted chameleons will be shaky and jittery when moving, occasionally suffering from tremors. They eventually develop bowed limbs, spinal deformities, bent casques, and soft

lower jaws. In advanced stages, most are unable to feed or use their tongue properly, behave listlessly, and lack an appetite.

This disease is usually caused by a lack of dietary calcium. If the animal's diet includes the proper amounts of calcium, other factors may be responsible; these factors include lack of vitamin D_3, inadequate UV-B exposure, inadequate heat, and inadequate vitamin supplementation.

The best course of treatment for an animal in the early stages of metabolic bone disease is to properly supplement its diet with a calcium/vitamin D_3 supplement, and to expose it to unfiltered sunlight (using the previously discussed methods) or an artificial UV-B light source. Provide adequate heat at all times. If your chameleon is weak, inactive, and unwilling to feed, consult a veterinarian.

Vitamin A Deficiency

The signs of vitamin A deficiency include puffy, teary, or crusted eyes; problems with shedding; sinus infections (small, pea-shaped lumps on top of the rostrum); respiratory problems; an inability to use the tongue; and a slow gait. Depending on the severity of your chameleon's symptoms, either treat the problem with proper vitamin A supplementation or consult a qualified veterinarian. Feed grated carrots, cooked yam, and other foods containing beta-carotene to your feeder insects before offering them to your chameleons.

This filarial worm was extracted from a panther chameleon.

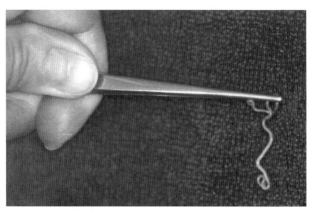

Neck, Throat, and Chest Edema

The signs of edema are a collar-like swelling of the neck, a localized swelling of the throat, or a lump-like swelling of the upper chest. Each of these symptoms may be caused by different diseases. Hypervitaminosis A or D (excessive amounts of either vitamin) is often the cause of neck edema, but not necessarily the cause of swelling in the throat or upper chest. These symptoms may be caused by hypothyroidism or hyperthyroidism, but such a possibility needs further investigation. Because temperature affects metabolic rate, it may also play a significant role.

Until more research is available, treatment remains speculative at best. Avoid high levels of vitamin D_3 and vitamin A supplementation, particularly with small, slow-growing montane species, and provide a basking site where your chameleons can achieve an optimal temperature.

Parasite and GI Tract Infections

Chameleons suffering from these problems may exhibit the following symptoms: weight loss, runny or discolored stools, listlessness, weakness, failure to feed (though some affected chameleons will eat a lot), and stools containing worms. Have a qualified veterinarian perform a fecal exam, diagnose the problem, and provide treatment. Do not use ivermectin on imported adult chameleons prone to filarial worm infections.

Subcutaneous Worms

Worm outlines are usually visible on the skin of afflicted chameleons. In most cases, these parasites are filarial worms, which are common among Malagasy chameleons, particularly panther chameleons. They are also common in some groups of Senegal chameleons. To treat the problem, make a small incision at the location of the worm and remove it with a fine pair of tweezers. Swab the incision with hydrogen peroxide; small incisions will close on their own in a short time. I recommend that you consult a veterinarian before attempting this procedure, because deep cuts can cause additional problems. The worms may also exist as microfilaria in the bloodstream. For young animals, this can be treated with ivermectin, but larger animals are best left untreated because of the high risk of death.

Mouth Infections

Signs of mouth infection include swelling along the gum line; yellow, caseous matter in the mouth; hard, black, scab-like matter protruding from the gumline in front of the mouth; difficulty feeding; and refusal to feed. If the caseous matter is easy to remove, clean out the site of infection and apply topical antibiotic solution or ointment. Increase the amount of vitamin C in your chameleon's diet, and make sure to provide adequate vitamin and mineral supplementation. Some mouth infections heal solely with the daily use of powdered or liquid vitamin C. If you have any doubt about your ability to deal with the infection, consult a qualified veterinarian.

Tongue Infection

Chameleons suffering from a tongue infection will not fully extend their tongue when feeding, and may cease feeding or using their tongue. In most cases, the tongue will appear swollen and/or the gular area will look distended. Consult a qualified veterinarian for treatment with antibiotics.

Shedding Problems

If your chameleon has difficulty shedding, or flaky or excessive shedding (do not confuse this with the normal, frequent shedding underwent by growing juveniles), it may be suffering from illness or dehydration. Excessive or inefficient vitamin supplementation also may be the culprit. Examine your husbandry methods and correct any problems. If your chameleon is sick, treat it.

Skin Problems

White skin bumps and dry, scaly patches can be caused by fungi or bacteria, but in some species, such as Jackson's and Meller's chameleons, they are usually fungal. These signs usually occur due to small skin punctures caused by overcrowding, or because of excessive humidity. Isolate infected animals and consult a veterinarian for treatment.

Swelling of Limbs

In imported animals, swollen limbs are sometimes the result of trauma suffered during collection. The swelling sometimes goes away on its own, but can be followed by secondary infections. Swollen limbs are also a sign of gout. If the swelling increases or does not disappear, consult a qualified veterinarian.

Tongue Hyperextension

After striking out after prey, your chameleon may be unable to retract its tongue. If this happens, place your chameleon in a bare tank with a single, low branch where it can perch, holding the animal and its tongue very carefully to prevent injury. Cover the bottom of the tank with moist paper towels or wet newspaper so that the chameleon's tongue does not dry out or become stuck. Do not use a heat pad or under-tank heater. To minimize stress and encourage muscular response, place the tank in a comfortably warm (around 75° F), dark area. Although this condition may look horrifying, a chameleon usually withdraw its tongue within twenty-four hours and returns to full normal function without additional intervention. Do not panic—it might cause irreparable damage. This condition is often associated with calcium deficiency.

Respiratory Infections

Gaping and puffing, accompanied by forced exhalations, are usually signs of respiratory infection. Often, these signs occur in tandem with an inflated body, loss of appetite, disinterest in basking, weakness, and closed or puffy eyes. If you think your chameleon is suffering from a respiratory infection, keep it at its optimal temperature, and consult a qualified veterinarian for proper treatment (usually an antibiotic). Gaping and forced exhalation are also signs other problems, including parasite infection.

Egg Binding

In certain gravid females, outlines of the eggs may remain visible though the female does not perform effective nest digging. These specimens often appear weak, have sunken eyes, and tend to stay at ground level, typically indicating that they are egg-bound.

To treat this condition, administer an easily absorbed source of calcium, such as calcium glubionate (Neocalglucon) once or twice each day. If a female is too weak to accept daily feedings, feed her a liquid diet (such as Ensure) or a thin mix of baby bird hand-feeding formula (Kaytee). Make sure that the chameleon does not choke on the liquid. To feed the chameleon, fill a syringe with the feeding formula, and slowly drip it on the front of its mouth until it begins to drink. Sometimes chameleons only begin drinking after they get a "taste" of the formula, which can be accomplished by pulling down the chameleon's lip and placing a drop on its gum, or by gently pulling down the gular skin and placing a single drop on its tongue. Never shoot the formula into the animal's mouth all at once. You can also avoid aspirating your chameleon by inserting a small syringe or feeding tube into its esophagus, but you should consult a qualified veterinarian before attempting this procedure. Continue to provide a suitable egg-laying site.

If your chameleon remains egg-bound, consult a veterinarian. Egg binding is a life-threatening condition, and happens more frequently among overfed, dehydrated, sick, and over-supplemented females. Lastly, do not confuse normal nest-seeking behavior with egg binding; gravid females may take several days, digging a number of test holes, before they lay their eggs.

Further Reading

For information on laws that regulate reptiles see Levell, J. P. Reptiles and the Law. Serpent's Tale. 1998. 612-470-5008.

INDEX

ABOUT THE AUTHOR

Philippe de Vosjoli is a highly acclaimed author of the best-selling reptile-care books, The Herpetocultural Library Series. His work in the field of herpetoculture has been recognized nationally and internationally for establishing high standards for amphibian and reptile care. His books, articles, and other writings have been praised and recommended by numerous herpetological societies, veterinarians, and other experts in the field. Philippe de Vosjoli was also the cofounder and president of The American Federation of Herpetoculturists, and was given the Josef Laszlo Memorial Award in 1995 for excellence in herpetoculture and his contribution to the advancement of the field.